D1698891

Brilliant As You Are!

Written by
PeTika Tave

Illustrated by
Vladimir Cebu, LL.B.

Copyright © 2020 by PeTika Tave

All rights reserved. This book or parts thereof may not be reproduced in any form, stored in any retrieval system, or transmitted in any form by any means—electronic, mechanical, photocopy, recording, or otherwise—without prior written permission of the publisher, except as provided by United States of America copyright law.
Published by BayaBooks and More
www.BAYABooks.com

Hardcover ISBN: 978-1-7341701-6-0
Paperback ISBN: 978-1-7341701-7-7
LCCN: 2020901657

To parents:

Children today are faced with so many images of society's definition of perfection – social media platforms, magazines, reality stars, TV idols – that they must learn to accept themselves for who they are, just the way they are. Start your child off with self-confidence as they venture into this sometimes unforgiving world with the *Beautiful (Brilliant) As You Are* (BAYA) collection.

Everything from peer pressure to self-doubt can lead children down a destructive path of depression and low self-esteem. Born from the author's desire to shield her own children from the negative effects of low self-confidence, the BAYA collection is dedicated to children of every size, shape, and color. Read these books to your child while they are still young and watch them blossom into the brilliant adult they are destined to become.

Each book has a special message of self-acceptance and self-love, to empower parents and give children the confidence they need to stand up to peer pressure and live fully in the skin they're in.

Look for more books to come at www.BayaBooks.com, but until then, remind your child daily of how brilliant they are, inside and out.

With Love,

PeTika

Dedication:

This book is dedicated to all the children who have found difficulty in loving who you are, just the way you are.

Having been tall and heavy my entire life, I want to give you the strength you need to love yourself. Know you're the perfect combination of everything that makes you, you. Not one mistake was made in your creation and it's so important that you believe in and love that.

Stand tall, be proud, regardless of who may want to hurt your feelings. Let no one break your spirit or make you cry tears of pain, for you are brilliant as you are, each and every day.

To my daughter Zee, born with immeasurable confidence and brilliance paralleled by none. This series was created to help children be strong and proud like you. I am so thrilled to be your mom.

To my son Ty, you too are my inspiration. Having dark-skin sometimes made you question your worth. I have watched you grow to love yourself and the body you are blessed with. Know that you are brilliant, just the way you are.

About the Author:

Being overweight and in the 99th percentile of kids for height all of her life, PeTika Tave struggled with self-love and acceptance for many years. Weighing in at 300 lbs. and six feet tall at the age of 13, the impact of low self-esteem was devastating. She spent her entire life dieting, reaching an all-time high of 427 lbs. at the age of 22. Near depression, emotional eating, low self-esteem, and no self-confidence, led her to make unhealthy choices that nearly cost her her life.

Vowing to be a better role model for her 1st child, she lost over 200 lbs. through healthy lifestyle changes and exercise. At the age of 29, while expecting her 2nd child, Ms. Tave started writing poetry to give her daughter, and other young girls, something she struggled with her entire life – a sense of self-worth. The BAYA collection started with that goal in mind. Now she is dedicated to inspiring children from every walk of life, using her career as a teacher to share wisdom and encouragement to help kids do and be their best.

The *Beautiful (Brilliant) As You Are* collection is designed to help parents empower their children with confidence so they can successfully navigate this thing called life.

Read lots, be well.

1

Young boy, you are **brilliant** as you are-

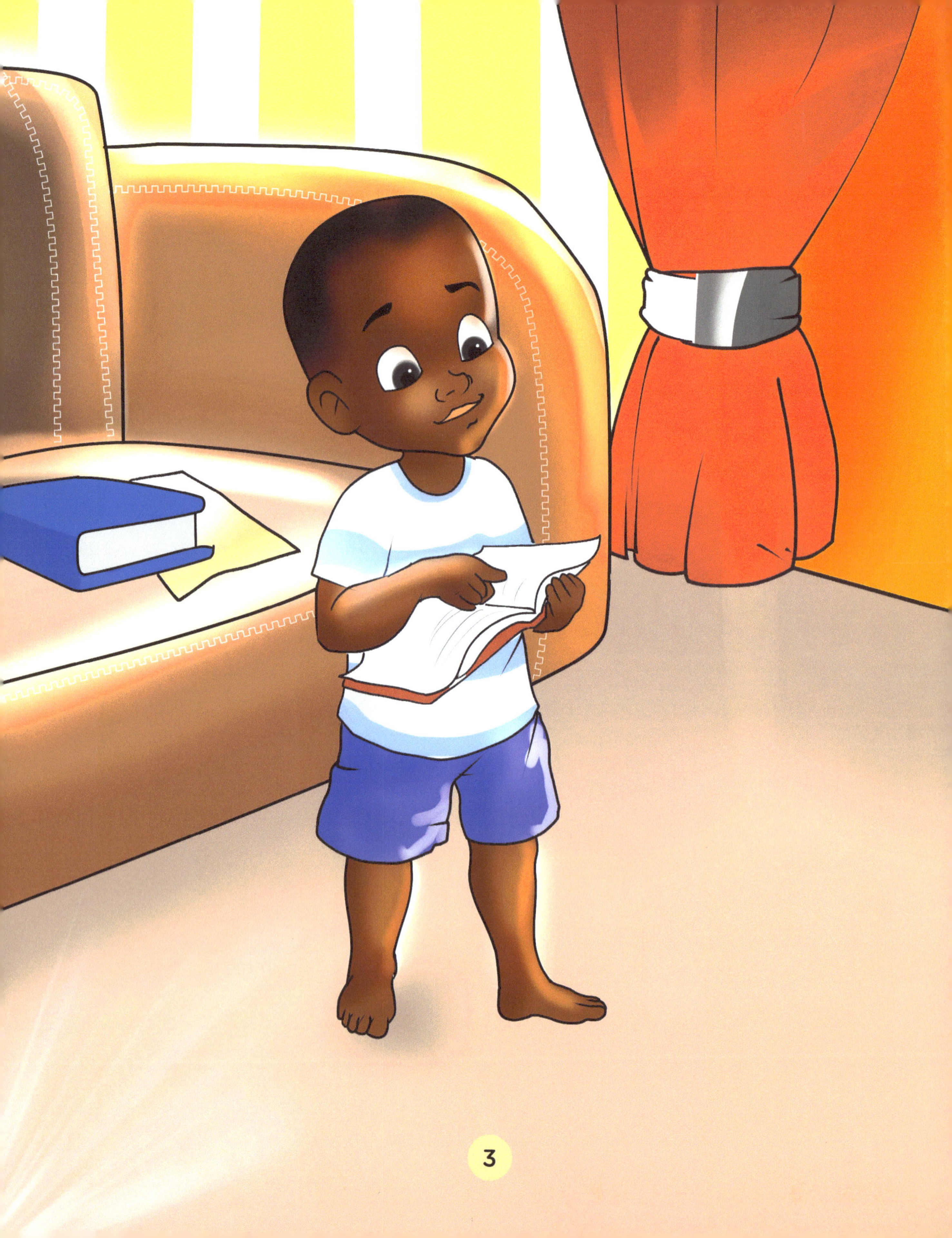

Handsome, curious, smart, creative.

5

Whether tall or short, **big** or thin, you are **wonderful** *as* you are because of *who* you are within.

7

You are not the pictures in a magazine, or the buffed-up people on a TV screen.

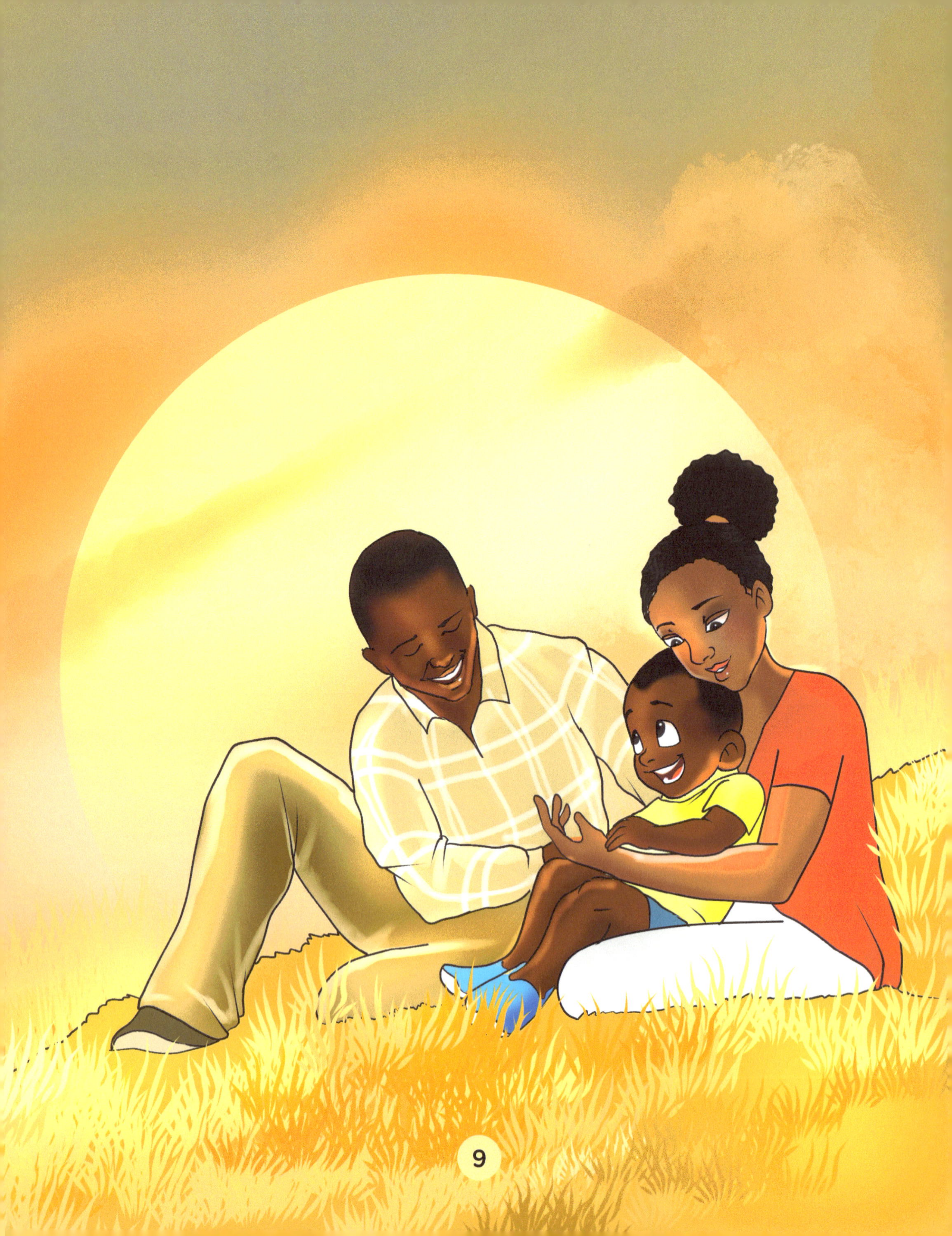

But you are a **prince** created with **love**.
You are the start of the man you'll become.

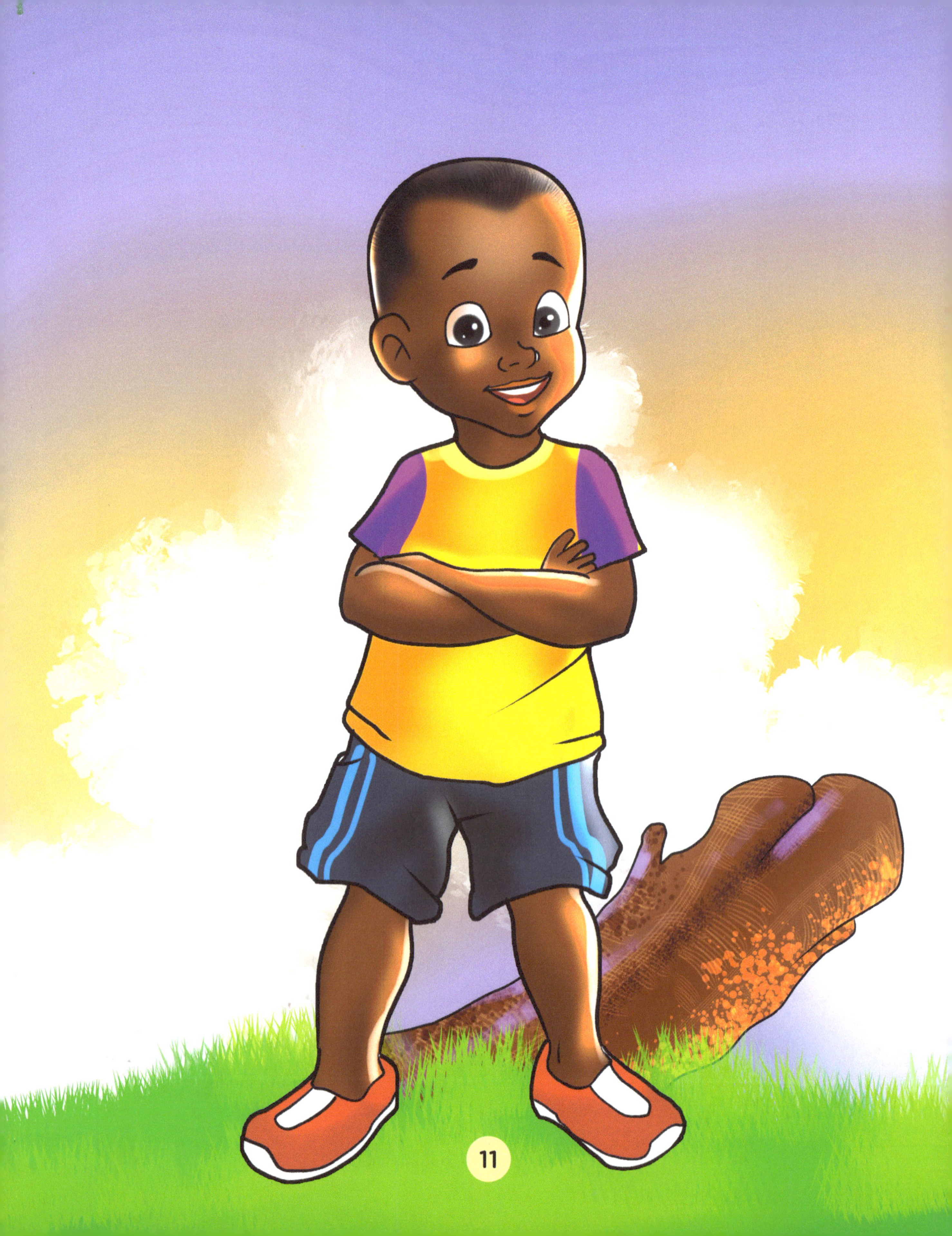

Perfect as you are in every little way, from the sound of your voice to the smile on your face.

Treasured young boy, don't worry any longer. Each day that you grow, makes you even **stronger**.

13

Walk tall, stand proud, believe in yourself.

Know you are **special**, listen to nothing less.

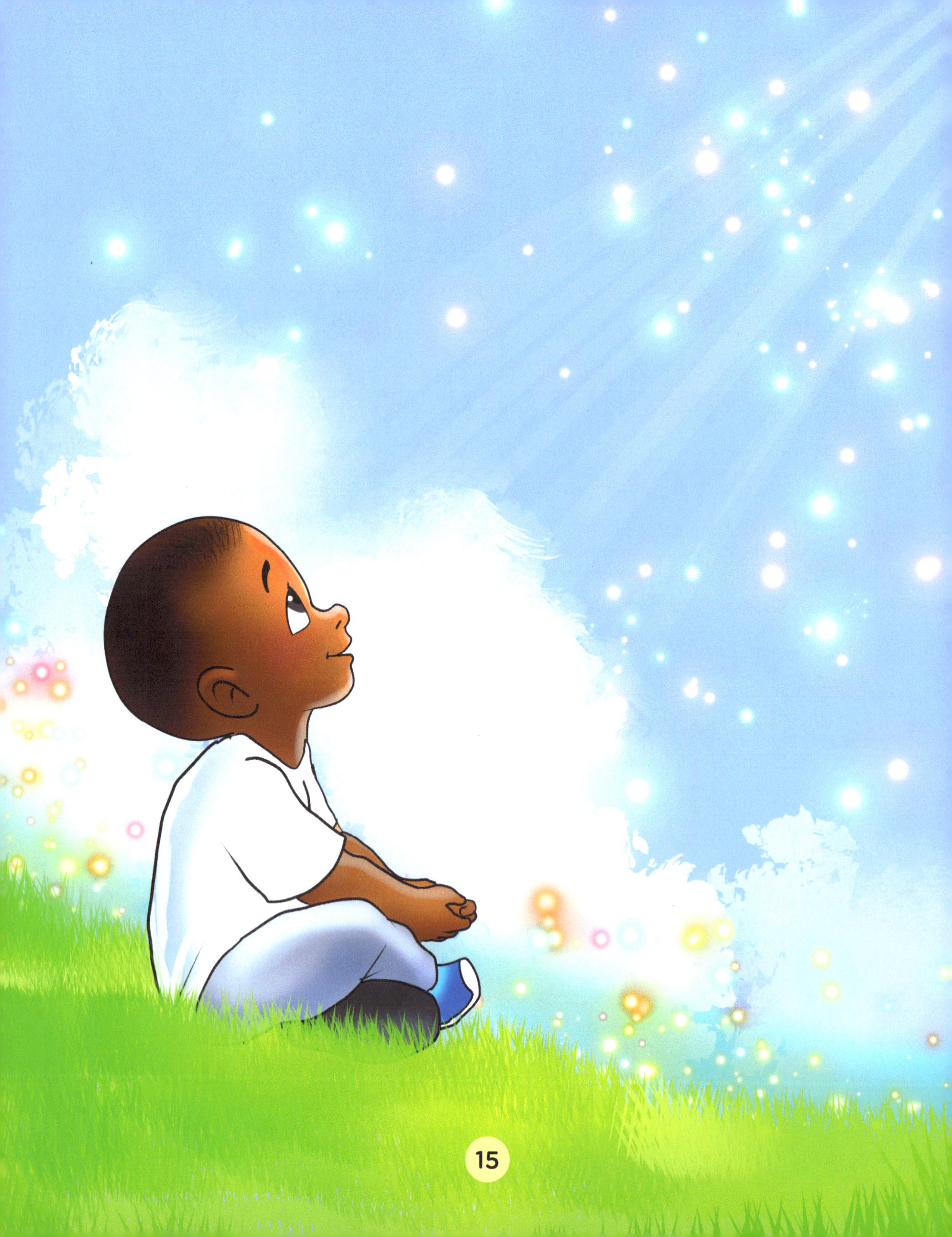

Always remember and know this to be true -

you are **brilliant as you are** because you're the one and only **YOU!**

The End.

Discussion Questions

As part of the *BAYA* mission, the goal of this series is to create confident children who stand proud in the skin they're in. To help parents have conversations about the topic, the following are suggested questions to spark an open discussion with your child:

1. What does it mean to be brilliant inside and out?

2. What makes you special?

3. What do you love about yourself?

4. Why is it important to be proud of who you are?

5. What does the author of the book want you to know?

I am **BRILLIANT** because ...

Use this page to make notes and draw pictures about what makes you brilliant. Write a message to yourself that you can read anytime you need a pick-me up, or attach your favorite pictures below and explain why you like them. This is your page, have fun!

Other titles
in the
BAYABooks collection

"Beautiful As You Are," a wonderful book that reminds young girls of how special they are. Available online and in select stores now. **Check it out!**

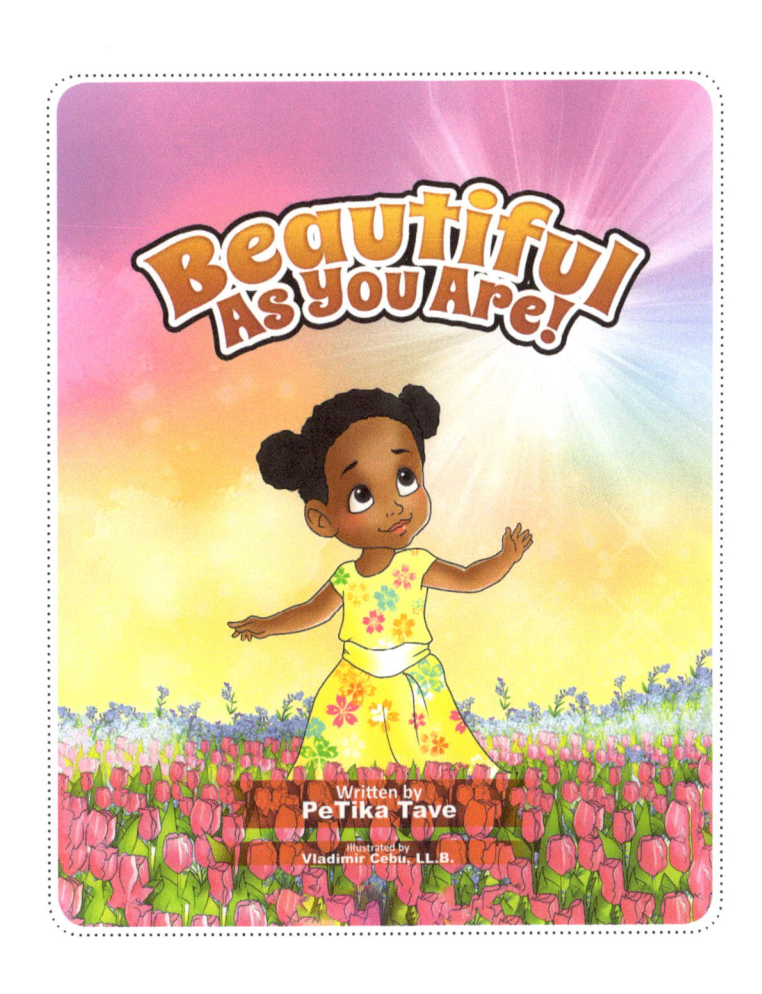

CPSIA information can be obtained
at www.ICGtesting.com
Printed in the USA
LVHW071754270320
651408LV00004B/11